ACHIEVING PEACE AT HOME

*LIFE CHANGING TOOLS TO
IMPROVE RELATIONSHIPS,
OVERHAUL THE WAY YOUR HOME OPERATES,
AND ACHIEVE LASTING PEACE.*

AMY MIKAL

CONTENTS

INTRODUCTION

AS AN AUTHOR WITH A HARD LEAN TOWARD SIMPLICITY and an appreciation for getting to the point, I believe as many readers will find this book surprising as I hope will find it accessible and easy to use. What I care about, and what I believe those of you who picked up this book want, is application. For many, this book will be a radical and challenging adventure in perspective. When you feel skeptical, I ask you to read on and give it a chance. If some of my scenarios don't feel relatable, I hope you can be gracious and creative as you contemplate your own. Of course, I look forward to lively conversations among readers as I know some of the concepts here will be challenging. I hope it sparks sincere discourse, innovation, and collaboration on the subject of peacemaking.

With regard to background and what qualifies me to write on this subject, I have been certified as a non-violent crisis intervention instructor, taught stress and anxiety management coursework at Northern Illinois University, and have completed training in interpersonal mediation. I participate in non-violent communication initiatives regularly. To be clear, I am not a licensed therapist or psychologist. I have studied the ideas and concepts in this book extensively because I care about them and because I have needed them in my own life. Like everyone else, I am a person in progress. The work of peacemaking is constant and I expect to be continually challenged, to experience both failure and success, as I strive to do that work.

I hope you love the book and that these concepts help you as they are helping me. I believe they are life changing and offer freedom. Most importantly, I truly believe in their power to heal and create a more peaceful world.

PART I:
THEORY

*A New Model for Achieving
Peace at Home*

CHAPTER 1
HOW WE FIRST EXPERIENCE AND IDENTIFY DISHARMONY

D ISHARMONY IS OFTEN CHARACTERIZED AS A CONFLICT or a fight but, long before we recognize it as a conflict, we are observing, experiencing, and probably exhibiting negative behaviors. Negative behaviors are our first clue that we, or those in our home, are struggling and that disharmony is present.

In the next several chapters, we will discuss how disharmony in our relationships originates, why it exists, and how to re-establish harmony so that you can experience lasting peace at home. This book is actionable and focused on application so, for those reasons, we will jump right in and begin with an activity that discusses negative behaviors you may be witnessing or exhibiting in your day to day life. For our purposes, we will be defining negative behaviors as any behavior that hurts or negatively impacts the self or others.

To start, I'm going to ask you to take a moment to consider any negative behaviors that may be affecting your life today or that have affected your life recently. Try to identify a scenario in your life that is only mildly irritating. These behaviors could be yours or someone else's. Don't pick an intense conflict you are involved in right now, as it may be too difficult to address for the purposes of this exercise. Find a mild example of negative behavior and, as you go through the rest of this chapter, keep this scenario in mind so that you have it to reflect on and refer back to.

Negative behaviors are often interpreted as an act of aggression. To create the peaceful home and life we desire, our view of negative behaviors needs to shift. We can do this by beginning to view negative behaviors as attempts to express or communicate. Rather than allowing the negative behaviors of others in our life to trigger us, we can try to adjust to experience the behaviors simply as information. The behavior is informing us about something that is going on in the life of the person exhibiting the behavior.

This is a radical shift in our approach and understanding of negative behaviors. The impulse to push back on this idea is not lost on me; however, when I talk about overhauling the way your home operates, it starts here.

It is our first and most difficult challenge because negative behaviors are often interpreted as disrespectful, rude, or malicious. Other words our culture uses in response to negative behaviors include disobedient, rebellious, attention-seeking (with a negative connotation), bad, trouble-making, etc. Though negative behaviors are often unproductive, ineffective, and even hurtful in their aim to communicate, they are none-the-less, attempts to communicate or express. Writing them off as flaws of character will certainly add to conflict in your home because such a response misses the reality of why the behavior is present.

Consider the possibility that behind every negative behavior is a feeling initiating that behavior. If you have a loved one who is exhibiting negative behaviors, that individual is experiencing a feeling that needs to be expressed. They may not have discerned an appropriate path for expressing their feeling, but there is information they are trying to share with you via that behavior.

One example might be a spouse who disengages after arriving home from work. We may interpret this behavior as unloving, disrespectful, or rude rather than looking for information about the condition of the person.

Disengaged/ Non-Communicative → Feeling mentally drained/ tired

Another example might be a parent who is being over-ly critical. We may have the tendency to vilify or create an "enemy image" of this person rather than looking for infor-mation about where their critical behavior is coming from or what it communicates about their current condition.

Feeling

Critical Comment   →   insecure/ not good enough

We can observe this dynamic in children, as well. When a child throws a "temper tantrum" because they did not get to sit in their favorite seat, it is common to interpret this as selfish, immature, or bad. Taking a moment to con-sider what information the child is trying to express via their behavior can provide insight into why this seat was so important to them, what losing it means to them, or if sitting in the seat is even related to the behavior at all.

Feeling

Temper Tantrum   →   unimportant/ sad/ isolated

We are talking about creating peace at home but these ideas relate to work scenarios as well. If a co-worker is drinking all the time and getting drunk every day after work, the negative behavior is informing us of other con-cerns occurring in the life of our co-worker. Rather than judging the situation as simply problematic, we can listen for information they may be trying to communicate via the behavior. We will be looking at a few models in upcoming chapters that suggest all behaviors are initiated by our feelings. We'll dive deeper into this concept and discuss how it can help us to reduce conflict in our lives and, help us to achieve lasting peace at home.

CHAPTER 1 EXERCISE:

Write down negative behaviors that you have observed. What feelings and information might these behaviors be trying to communicate?

_____

_____

_____

_____

_____

_____

_____

CHAPTER 2
UNDERSTANDING NEGATIVE BEHAVIORS

W E HAVE TALKED ABOUT HOW NEGATIVE BEHAVIORS present themselves as a way of communicating information. What could the individuals exhibiting these behaviors possibly be trying to communicate with their behavior other than hurt and confusion?

According to Dr. Nicholas Long, a founder of *Life Space Crisis Intervention* and developer of the Conflict Cycle (a model that demonstrates the cyclical and escalating nature of conflict), we behave and act according to the feelings we are having or are needing to express. We might share a word of encouragement with a friend when we are feeling great and we might share a critical word when we are feeling insecure.

I'm a firm believer that humans want to think well of themselves and therefore do not enjoy hurting others (even when they say they do). We want to like who we are.

We want to like ourselves. So, when we behave negatively, it is not usually enjoyable, or at least not in the long run. Much of the time, we may not be reflective enough to understand why we are even behaving in such a way. We may want to communicate something but, as we have no idea how to communicate it properly, it comes out in the form of negative behaviors. We may not even be completely aware of what the problem is. It is very helpful to have an observer who can see our behavior as an attempt to express and who can respectfully investigate further to help us communicate our feelings and concerns in a productive way.

Having the language to communicate how we are feeling can be incredibly helpful in reducing negative behaviors and conflict. To assist people in expressing their feelings, the Center for Non-Violent Communication has developed a feelings inventory that can be a great communication tool.

FEELINGS WHEN YOUR NEEDS ARE NOT SATISFIED:

Angry
enraged
furious
incensed
indignant
irate
livid
outraged
resentful

Annoyed
aggravated
dismayed
disgruntled
displeased
exasperated
frustrated
impatient
irritated
irked

Aversion
animosity
appalled
contempt
disgusted
dislike
hate
horrified
hostile
repulsed

Afraid
apprehensive
dread
foreboding
frightened
mistrustful
panicked
petrified
scared
suspicious
terrified
wary
worried

Disquiet
agitated
alarmed
discombobulated
disconcerted
disturbed
perturbed
rattled
restless
shocked
startled
surprised
troubled
turbulent
turmoil
uncomfortable
uneasy
unnerved
unsettled
upset

Disconnected
alienated
aloof
apathetic
bored
cold
detached
distant
distracted
indifferent
numb
removed
uninterested
withdrawn

Confused
ambivalent
baffled
bewildered
dazed
hesitant
lost
mystified
perplexed
puzzled
torn

(c) 2005 by Center for Nonviolent Communication Website: www. cnvc.org Email: cnvc@cnvc.org Phone: 1.505.244.4041

(Cont.)

Embarrassed

ashamed
chagrined
flustered
guilty
mortified
self-conscious

Fatigue

beat
burnt out
depleted
exhausted
lethargic
listless
sleepy
tired
weary
worn out

Pain

agony
anguished
bereaved
devastated
grief
heartbroken
hurt
lonely
miserable
regretful
remorseful

Sad

depressed
dejected
despair
despondent
disappointed
discouraged
disheartened
forlorn
gloomy
heavy hearted
hopeless
melancholy
unhappy
wretched

Tense

anxious
cranky
distressed
distraught
edgy
fidgety
frazzled
irritable
jittery
nervous
overwhelmed
restless
stressed out

Vulnerable

fragile
guarded
helpless
insecure
leery
reserved
sensitive
shaky

Yearning

envious
jealous
longing
nostalgic
pining
wistful

When we observe a negative behavior, we can ask, "Are you feeling...?" or we can share this list of feelings with others to help them communicate with words rather than with negative behavior.

> "I feel *depleted* when I get home and need time to rest before talking."

> "I am feeling *troubled* because things at work are not going well."

Understanding that feelings inform behavior is the first step to reducing conflict in your home. This concept is demonstrated in LSCI's Conflict Cycle (Img. 1). The model expresses the cyclical nature of conflict as it escalates into a crisis when intervention does not occur.

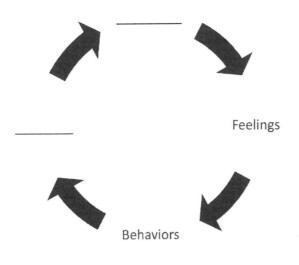

Feelings

Behaviors

Img.1 *LSCI Conflict Cycle*

The next time you and your partner find yourselves arguing over some behavior, step back for a moment and consider what feelings might be motivating their side of the issue. Heck, ask them directly. What feelings are behind the behavior?

If you receive a critical remark from your parent, try to pause before responding and consider if they might be feeling insecure about something. Did something just happen that may have contributed to their feeling insecure? Criticism is often present where feelings of insecurity exist.

If your child is escalating and appears to be getting more dramatic over an issue, try to remember to check in with them before responding to their behavior. They may be feeling disconnected, apprehensive, frustrated, or embarrassed about something. Work to understand what they are feeling and address the feeling rather than the behavior. When a child understands that their concerns will be heard and honored, behavior problems dramatically decrease.

Dealing with a co-worker's frustrating behavior can also be made a bit easier by working to understand the emotions present behind their behavior. Perhaps they are nervous about a presentation or getting a project done before a deadline. Their feelings will definitely be contributing to the behavior that is driving you up the wall and understanding those feelings can help you to cope with the situation.

FEELINGS WHEN YOUR NEEDS ARE SATISFIED

Affectionate

compassionate
friendly
loving
open hearted
sympathetic
tender
warm

Engaged

absorbed
alert
curious
engrossed
enchanted
entranced
fascinated
interested
intrigued
involved
spellbound
stimulated

Exhilarated

blissful
ecstatic
elated
enthralled
exuberant
radiant
rapturous
thrilled

Excited

amazed
animated
ardent
aroused
astonished
dazzled
eager
energetic
enthusiastic
giddy
invigorated
lively
passionate
surprised
vibrant

Inspired

amazed
awed
wonder

Joyful

amused
delighted
glad
happy
jubilant
pleased
tickled

Grateful

appreciative
moved
thankful
touched

Peaceful

calm
clear headed
comfortable
centered
content
equanimous
fulfilled
mellow
quiet
relaxed
relieved
satisfied
serene
still
tranquil
trusting

Hopeful

expectant
encouraged
optimistic

Refreshed

enlivened
rejuvenated
renewed
rested
restored
revived

Confident

empowered
open
proud safe
secure

Lastly, it can be just as helpful to have words that describe our feelings when things are going well.

> "When you encourage me to go back to school, I feel *empowered* to achieve my dreams."

> "I'm sorry I accidentally knocked the lamp off of your table. I was feeling *exuberant!*"

We have discussed the idea that behaviors come from feelings but, from where do feelings come? Why do they exist? What purpose do they serve? In the next chapter, we'll discuss how and from where our feelings arise. This is the second step to overhauling your home and achieving lasting peace.

CHAPTER 2 EXERCISE:

Identify 3 scenarios in which you observed negative behaviors. Again, avoid highly emotional scenarios as you may not be ready to work through them at this time. Let at least one of the scenarios involve your own negative behaviors. Once you have identified the three scenarios, take time to consider what emotions might have been influencing those behaviors. Write down your hypothesis for each scenario. Of course, without consulting the people in your scenarios, your hypothesis may not be accurate; however, beginning to connect behavior with emotion is important.

_____

_____

_____

_____

_____

CHAPTER 3
THE ORIGIN OF FEELINGS

THERE IS A LOT OF DEBATE OVER WHERE FEELINGS/ emotions originate, whether they are reliable, and what purpose they serve. Are they instinctual or chosen? A strength or a weakness?

For our purposes, we are going to focus on the helping nature of emotions and how they can be used to inform us and others about a situation. According to the LSCI Conflict Cycle, feelings, especially negative ones, originate with a stressful event or an anxious thought. Our thoughts induce feelings which are expressed, if not verbally, via behavior (Img. 2).

Refer back to a scenario where you witnessed negative behaviors. If those behaviors were an expression of a feeling, and that feeling was caused by a stressful event or an anxious thought, what might the event or thought have been? You may have some indication based on the situation or you may have no idea. Feelings are influenced by thoughts whether those thoughts are rational or not, conscious or unconscious.

Feeling distraught over the thought of losing one's pet when a terminal diagnosis has been received, is rational. Feeling abandoned when your partner leaves for a work trip, is not rational; however, the feeling of abandonment may be real and can therefore, affect behavior. We might be totally aware of the thoughts behind our feelings or we could experience feelings without knowing or exploring exactly what thoughts or events initiated them.

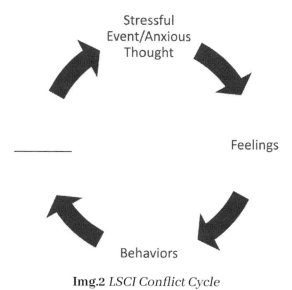

Img.2 *LSCI Conflict Cycle*

Anxious thoughts and stressful events often revolve around needs that we have. Not getting our needs met causes everyone significant amounts of anxiety. To help individuals identify where their feelings are coming from and what their anxious thoughts are about, a list of our human needs can be a useful tool.

The following is a list of needs identified by the Center for Non-Violent Communication.

ALL HUMANS HAVE A NEED FOR:

Connection

acceptance
affection
appreciation
belonging
cooperation
communication
closeness
community
companionship
compassion
consideration
consistency
empathy
inclusion
intimacy
love
mutuality
nurturing
respect/self-respect
safety
security
stability
support
to know and be known
to see and be seen
to understand and be understood
trust
warmth

Physical Wellbeing

air
food
movement/exercise
rest/sleep
sexual expression
safety
shelter
touch
water

Play

joy
humor

Honesty

authenticity
integrity
presence

Autonomy

choice
freedom
independence
space
spontaneity

Meaning

awareness
celebration of life
challenge
clarity
competence
consciousness
contribution
creativity
discovery
efficacy
effectiveness
growth
hope
learning
mourning
participation
purpose
self-expression
stimulation
to matter
understanding

Peace

beauty
communion
ease
equality
harmony
inspiration
order

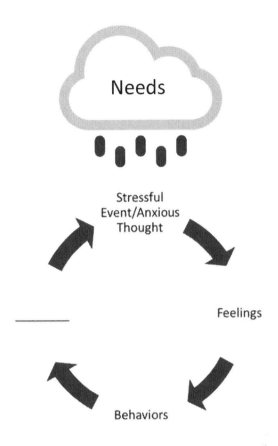

Img.3 *The Peaceful Home Model (LSCI Conflict Cycle; needs added by author)*

In seeking to establish a peaceful home, our primary concern is that unchecked anxious thoughts, and unaddressed stressful events, will likely escalate. Negative feelings and behaviors (or as we now know them—attempts to communicate) will continue.

We cannot expect to meet all of the needs of our family members, but we can help them to identify, communicate, and express their needs. If we can help to meet a need, great! If not, we can work with and problem solve together to help everyone get their needs met via alternative, and more productive, ways.

SCENARIO 1

When a child throws a temper tantrum because they did not get to sit in their preferred seat, there may be something deeper happening. Dismissing the negative behavior as selfish or bad can escalate the situation. We can ask how they are feeling and what thoughts they are having that might be creating those feelings. An example might be, "I'm feeling sad because they always get the good seat." Children will often give shallow or pat answers because they do not yet know how to express all they may be thinking or feeling. Patiently investigating the child's true concerns can help to bring quick resolution to the situation. Are they feeling disconnected from you and therefore sad? Are they feeling less important than other children? Do they need time to receive positive attention? Perhaps there is a fear of sitting near someone else for a legitimate reason. Once the need is identified, a reassuring conversation can be had about how and when we will work together to meet that need.

In caring for children, there is often a great deal of emphasis placed on the child's physical needs but, viewing our needs list, we see that so many more of our human needs fall outside of that category!

It can be very emotional to voice a need that one has never been able to voice before. When we finally have words and permission to share them, it is freeing but it can be scary. Understanding and using this model at home can dramatically change the environment in your home. It will bring freedom to your family—as long as individuals feel safe to share their needs.

Feelings are critical as they tell us about our needs. A home where feelings and needs are suppressed is not a safe home. Negative behaviors will present in a desperate attempt to meet those needs.

SCENARIO 2

Another example of identifying the origin of feelings might be understanding the anxiety behind our feelings of anger when another driver crosses the line and cuts us off on the highway. The feeling of anger tells us something is wrong. It is initiated by anxiety and it tells us that we have a need that is not being met. What is our need in this scenario? A need for safety! Being cut off is a stressful event because we are responsible for our own safety and someone has just stepped in, or literally crossed over, and interfered with our efforts to remain safe. Of course, this event causes feelings of anger. But what is our next move? Those feelings of anger may lead to negative behaviors on our part. How will we stop the Conflict Cycle from continuing?

SCENARIO 3

A co-worker blames you for their inability to complete their project. You understand that this action is motivated by their own anxiety. Perhaps they are worried about their relationship with the boss or about losing respect for not having their project done on time. Whatever their anxiety, it has motivated their negative behavior of blaming you for the situation. You now have a choice. Will you react to their behavior with anxiety of your own? Will you allow your own anxiety to influence your behavior in a negative direction? Or will you respond to their negative behavior in a way that de-escalates the situation?

In the next chapter, we discuss how the conflict cycle continues, escalates, or is ended.

CHAPTER 3 EXERCISE:

Identify 3 scenarios in which you observed negative behaviors. Again, avoid highly emotional scenarios as you
may not be ready to work through them at this time. Let
at least one of the scenarios involve your own negative behaviors. Once you have identified the three scenarios, take
time to consider what emotions and what anxieties might
have been influencing those behaviors. Might a stressful
event have preceded the behaviors? An anxious thought?
Write down your hypothesis for each scenario and what
unmet needs that person may have. Of course, without
consulting the people in your scenarios, your hypothesis
may not be accurate; however, beginning to connect emotion with anxiety is important.

_____

_____

_____

_____

_____

_____

_____

_____

_____

_____

_____

CHAPTER 4
RESPONDING TO NEGATIVE BEHAVIORS

N THE LAST FEW CHAPTERS, WE CONSIDERED SEVERAL different conflict scenarios where individuals were experiencing some amount of disharmony in their lives. How do these conflicts escalate and turn into a crisis? A crisis can mean any sort of traumatic event or situation ranging from a temper tantrum or serious argument to a physical altercation or mental illness. A crisis can also look like a job loss, a broken marriage, or a criminal action. When we refer to crisis, we are referring to what can result from a conflict cycle that has not been interrupted and stopped. It has escalated into something much larger than the initial conflict (See Img. 4).

If another driver cuts you off and you respond with your own negative behavior, will the conflict escalate or de-escalate? Most likely, it will escalate. The final event in the LSCI Conflict Cycle model is how others respond to witnessed behaviors.

Img.4 *The Peaceful Home Model (LSCI Conflict Cycle; needs added by author)*

If others respond to an anxious person's behavior in a positive, caring, and supportive way, the cycle can be ended. However, if the response of others is negative, judgmental, unsupportive, or reactive (or interpreted as so), the conflict will continue and will likely escalate. It can cycle over and over again until a full-blown crisis is at hand.

One individual's negative behavior can initiate anxiety or trauma in others, as well. In this case, the cycle expands. Considering the dynamic here, we see the great challenge that is before us when we seek to establish peace and, the courage required to de-escalate a conflict situation. If another's behavior initiates our own anxiety and our own concern about not having needs met, we have a decision to make. Can we overcome our anxiety and consider the unmet needs of the other or, do we need to retreat for a time to manage our own anxiety and focus on self-care?

THE GOOD/BAD NARRATIVE

In many cultures, negative behavior is viewed as an indication of bad character, low morals, a sinful nature, or evil intent. Images of old movies come to mind where the "good guy" is dressed in all white and the "bad guy" is dressed in all black. In this perspective, the nature of an individual is judged according to their behavior. Individuals engaged in negative behaviors may be accused of having evil or selfish intentions.

When we view negative behavior as a dysfunctional attempt to meet one's needs, however, or as a dysfunctional attempt to managing our anxiety, the good/bad narrative is pulled into question. Is this an evil or selfish individual or, is this a desperate/anxious individual? Which one is it? What we believe about the individual will drastically impact our response to their behavior and, it will drastically impact whether or not the conflict cycle escalates or is stopped. When we believe that behavior reflects personal nature, we judge the person. When we believe that behavior reflects personal need, we are more likely to be compassionate and to unlock peace.

This is a very hard concept to accept. We want to set ourselves apart from "bad people." This separation is often a tool we use to define and protect ourselves. We use it to feel good about ourselves. Sometimes to meet our own needs for self-respect or self-worth. It can be extremely difficult to acknowledge the humanity of someone who has hurt us or others deeply. It can be difficult to imagine their own anxieties and understand their attempts to protect, however misguided. If someone has a need to be heard about a very serious matter but their attempts to be heard have failed repeatedly, the individual's anxiety is going to escalate while they continue to try to find ways to be heard. Unfortunately, if they do not find a successful way to be heard, they may resort to negative behaviors in attempting to meet this need. This does not condone the negative behavior. Though sometimes effective, it is most likely dysfunctional and hurtful to the individual and to others. The negative behavior does represent, however, the individual's attempt to express an unmet need and their ignorance about how to do so in a functional, positive, and effective way.

We do not typically judge an individual, trying to meet a need and to reduce their anxiety, as bad. However, if an individual is using a dysfunctional strategy to meet their need, we often allow that strategy to define them. In reality, they may have been unable to identify a more functional strategy in their desperation to meet the need. They may be putting all of their energy into meeting other needs and struggling to meet this one in a functional way.

This is often an issue of education. Education about how to meet our own needs and how to reduce our own anxiety in a way that is functional (effective without injury to self or others), is *critical*.

If labeled in negative ways often enough, some individuals come to believe these ideas about themselves—that they are bad or evil. If they have experienced repeated failures to meet their own needs, or have resorted to negative behaviors to meet them, they may concede to the negative narrative and agree with negative labels. In addition, if the response of self to one's own behavior is judgmental and unforgiving, this can contribute to anxiety, self-sabotage, and perpetuating one's internal conflict.

ESCALATING RESPONSES

What are some responses to behaviors that may escalate a conflict? If a child is throwing a tantrum because they are feeling less important than a sibling, will telling them they are naughty or overly sensitive meet their need for connection? Or, will it escalate the child's feelings of disconnection and contribute to their anxiety about personal value? If we are feeling overwhelmed at work and having difficulty completing a task, will making our boss feel bad about what they've asked us to do escalate or de-escalate the situation? If your sister tells you about an event that scared her, will minimizing or dismissing her story escalate or de-escalate the situation? Our responses to another individual's expressed anxiety, have a huge impact on the direction of the conversation and the relationship. Antagonizing, minimizing, mocking, ignoring, shaming, yelling, etc.—these will all escalate an individual's anxiety and likely negative behaviors. Escalating responses typically focus on the behavior rather than the anxiety behind the behavior.

EXAMPLES OF ESCALATING RESPONSES:

- I can't believe how selfish you are.
- You should be ashamed of yourself.
- That was a dumb thing to do.

- You are being rebellious.
- What is your problem?
- What's wrong with you?
- Your concern is not important.
- I don't care what you do.
- I don't have time to listen.
- You'll get over it.
- Stop making a big deal out of it.
- You look ridiculous when you behave that way.
- You are being very immature.
- This is classic you...

DE-ESCALATING RESPONSES

Responding to expressed anxiety and negative behaviors with compassion and concern for an individual (or group) can quickly put out the flame of conflict. Learning about and addressing their anxieties directly and with respect, will leave the other party feeling cared for. A de-escalating response typically focuses on the anxiety behind the behavior rather than on the behavior itself. Expressing concern about their needs and how they will get their needs met drastically lowers anxiety. Even if we are unable to meet an individual's needs, knowing that we care about them and want to help them get their needs met is enough to eliminate conflict and build stronger relationships.

EXAMPLES OF DE-ESCALATING RESPONSES:

- Your concerns are important to me.
- I see this issue is important to you. Can you tell me more about it and why?
- I see you are upset, are you feeling anxious about something?
- I'm sorry to see you upset. How can I help?
- This behavior is not working. What are some better ways to get your need for _____, met?
- I understand you are upset, let's find a way to help you get your need for __ met.
- If you are concerned about something, I would prefer we talk about it.
- I understand you are concerned about ____. That is important to me, too. Perhaps we can meet that need in a different way.
- This behavior is not working. Let's talk about what's bothering you.
- Let's think of some ways to meet that need without hurting yourself or others.
- I noticed some avoidance. Are you concerned about something?

CHAPTER 4 EXERCISE:

Take a moment to re-write the responses below so that they are de-escalating.

Hurry up, you are making me late!

_____

_____

_____

I don't have time to listen.

_____

_____

_____

Stop making a big deal out of it.

_____

_____

_____

You should be ashamed of yourself.

_____

_____

_____

A recent escalating response I had and how I will respond differently next time:

_____

_____

_____

CHAPTER 5
RETRACING NEGATIVE BEHAVIORS

NOW THAT WE HAVE REVIEWED THE ELEMENTS IN-volved in LSCI's Conflict Cycle, and the needs behind the anxieties that feed it, we can turn our attention to prevention. The first and most important step in preventing a conflict, or stopping its escalation, is to recognize it via observed behaviors. This may initially look like an expressed concern, a behavior, or a simple comment. How we or others respond to that first communication is key. We want to start by retracing what we have just observed.

The second step, is to address a stressful event that may have occurred prior to the negative behavior or, to address an anxious thought that may or may not have been expressed. It is sometimes a delicate conversation when you seek to understand another person's anxiety. They may be ashamed of their anxiety or, they may not even be aware of it themselves. They may be feeling insecure and not want you to know. Use discretion and consider the type of relationship you have with the individual. To begin addressing their concerns, it can be helpful to simply ask, "how are you feeling about what just happened?" or "How does _____ make you feel?" Sometimes the individual's basic feelings are obvious—sad, angry, frustrated, etc. In these cases, you can move directly to trying to understand their anxious thoughts about the situation. If interacting with an employer, potential inquiries might be, "What are your primary concerns on this matter?" or, "What concerns do you have that I should keep in mind?" In other situations, asking, "Are you feeling anxious or concerned about anything in particular?" or, "Do you have a need for something that is not being met?" A simple, "Is something bothering you?" or "It seems like you have some concerns on your mind," can open up conversation and allow the individual to express their anxieties about specific needs without a conflict developing. Accepting and supporting their emotions is important to build trust and to instill confidence in their resilience as it relates to their concern.

The following is a scenario that reviews the relationship between behavior, emotion, anxiety and disharmony:

Jimmy is in second grade and is anxious about making friends. Not only is he anxious about this but, learning how to build social connections is a developmental task that he has a need to meet. Social connections are very high on his priority list at this age. Because he is anxious about this, he takes advantage of an opportunity to connect with another child in his classroom who has just reached out to him (even though it means talking while the teacher is talking). Because Jimmy chooses an inappropriate strategy to meet his need for connection, Jimmy is reprimanded and his name is written on the board under "no recess." Jimmy experiences the following feelings and anxieties when he sees his name on the board:

- Humiliation (the whole class sees my name on the board under "no recess")
- Anxious about being labeled a "bad kid"
- Mis-understood motives (not trying to distract or disrespect; trying to connect)
- Anxious self-hatred (I can't trust myself to keep myself out of trouble; I make stupid mistakes; I let myself down; I don't know how to get my needs met in an appropriate way)

Jimmy arrives home that evening and is anxious about his parents' response. Because of his anxiety, he is avoidant and he is short when others speak to him. At dinner, his parents reprimand him for being short with his sister. Jimmy experiences the following feelings and anxieties when he is reprimanded:

- Anger (I can't do anything right)
- They think I'm a bad kid
- Mis-understood motives (not trying to hurt sister; trying to avoid attention and protect self)
- Anxious self-hatred (failed at protecting self; I make stupid mistakes)

Jimmy's negative behaviors will likely continue if others' responses to his behavior do not address his underlying anxieties—primarily how to meet his own need for acceptance and peer connection. Unfortunately, this conflict has the potential to cycle and escalate over time and can even result in Jimmy believing negative labels and self-identifying as a "bad kid" or "trouble."

By looking past his behaviors to the anxieties behind them, Jimmy's community has a much greater chance at successfully ending the conflict and supporting Jimmy's positive self-image.

Let's retrace the negative behavior in this scenario from the parent's perspective to identify what initiated the behavior:

Observed behavior:

- An expression of anger at the dinner table

What preceded the expression of anger?

- A reprimand from parents
- Anxious thoughts
- Feeling not good enough

What preceded the reprimand?

- Short responses to his sister
- Avoidant behavior

What preceded the short responses and avoidant behavior?

- Getting in trouble at school
- Anxious thoughts
- Feelings of humiliation, sadness

What preceded getting in trouble at school?

- Talking during class/ An attempt at connection

What preceded talking during class?

- **Anxiety** about making friends and meeting his need for connection

If Jimmy's community had recognized the presence of a conflict or concern via the observed behavior (step 1), and addressed Jimmy's anxious thoughts or unexpressed needs (step 2), the potential to end the conflict quickly, would have been much higher. Additionally, Jimmy's positive self-image would more likely remain intact.

This may sound like we are making a lot of assumptions about Jimmy's needs and anxieties; however, when we judge a person's intent and character by their observed behavior, and punish them for it, we make assumptions as well. We are more often inclined to assume the worst when we observe negative behavior rather than the best. We sometimes say, "oh, they should know better," but unfortunately, even adults do not always know how to meet their own needs in effective and appropriate ways.

Does this mean that we don't address the problems created by negative behaviors? No. If inappropriate or dysfunctional strategies are used to meet our needs, the natural consequences of those negative behaviors are important lessons. They teach us to find more appropriate ways of getting our needs met. This is very different from punishment. A natural consequence does not speak to the nature of an individual, whereas, punishment tends to infer a "badness" and deleterious intent thereby judging an individual's personal nature. The goal here is to treat individuals exhibiting negative behaviors with respect and, to assist them in maintaining self-respect by sharing positive and effective strategies for meeting needs. Loss of respect from others or self is a huge anxiety that is at play in many, if not all, of our conflicts.

CHAPTER 5 EXERCISE:

Take a moment to recall a recent stressful event. Do not select an extremely stressful event, but something mild that will help you to apply these concepts without elevating your anxiety. What were some of the feelings and behaviors you noticed following the event? What needs were unmet?

_____

_____

_____

What responses to these feelings and behaviors would be supportive and de-escalating?

_____

_____

_____

PART II: PRACTICE

Applying the
Peaceful Home Model

CHAPTER 6
ACHIEVING PEACE AT HOME

THERE ARE A FEW WAYS YOU CAN BEGIN TO APPLY THE concepts in this book to your life and to overhaul the way your home operates to achieve lasting peace. Before we get into those strategies, let's identify a few foundational items that a peaceful home must have to begin the work. A peaceful home requires that we be ready to use the following:

Intention

A willingness to engage and to do the work that peace requires is necessary. Peace is not a passive process. When we talk about peace, we are not referring to the day when we finally all agree or when we finally influence someone to our way of thinking. Peace requires that we move toward the middle, that we step toward our differences, and that we express a willingness to work to understand things as others understand them.

Courage

As we allow ourselves to listen to others with different perspectives, we open ourselves up to new ideas and may feel very vulnerable. We may experience a fear of being misled, of being wrong, or of instability in our world resulting from our need for honesty, reliability, and stability. If any of our needs feel threatened, we can quickly put up our protective barriers (often negative behaviors). It takes courage to listen and be open to a new idea that we may feel threatens our ability to meet needs.

Attention

Paying attention to those around us and what they are trying to express, is critical if we are to create a healthy foundation for a peaceful home. It is helpful to delay our responses to behavior and be attentive to what an individual may be trying to express through their behavior. Remembering that most behavior is an attempt to communicate.

Empathy

It is difficult to connect with an individual's need if we are unable to consider how we might feel if we were having their same experience. Because feelings point to stressful events or anxious thoughts, we need to be able to consider how we might feel, and therefore think, in a particular situation.

Communication

Expressing sincere concern for unmet needs, and a desire to help problem solve to meet them, is foundational to the establishment of lasting peace within your home.

Once these foundational pieces are in place, you can focus on introducing the concepts from this book into your home and prepare to be amazed by the changes and lasting peace you experience.

Sometimes, when we want to make a major change in our lives, it is helpful to plan time and space to declare the change and to invite others to join. Perhaps apologies are in order or requests for support. *Establishing a dedicated time to share concerns in a safe space, without judgement or criticism, is helpful.*

It may also be beneficial to establish ground rules for how people will be treated in your home. Identify boundaries and highlight natural consequences. Re-iterate your concern for others and your desire to help them get their needs met. Acknowledge that you cannot meet everyone's needs yourself but that you are willing to problem solve with them to help them get their needs met through other means. Discuss collaboration and what that means to you and those you love.

Taking the time to communicate your desire to improve your relationships is rarely unappreciated and, letting others know that their needs and concerns are important to you can be more healing than you may know.

If you do not feel comfortable declaring a major change in how your home is going to operate, another approach could be to begin slowly applying these concepts on your own and in your daily interactions. Observe behaviors present in your relationships and slowly begin to investigate what needs are being expressed through those behaviors. You can allow change to happen organically as you improve your ability to apply these concepts in your relationships. Let those around you know you care about their needs. Let yourself know you care about your own needs.

A third way to begin applying these concepts in your life is to keep a journal of dis-harmonious events and reconciliations. You can record the breakdown of each event to find the root anxiety or stressful event and identify unmet needs. This can be a very beneficial daily practice as you strengthen your peacemaking muscles and grow in compassion.

If you come across a situation where it seems that sharing your own unmet need will not be taken well, it may be time to clarify or redefine that relationship. If someone is getting their needs met at your expense, without your willing participation, you may want to reconsider the type of relationship or level of closeness you share with that person. A conversation may resolve it but, if not, some boundary setting to ensure you are able to get your needs met, is appropriate. *For assistance with understanding and setting boundaries in your relationships, look for the recommended resources at the back of this book.*

CHAPTER 6 EXERCISE:

List three actions you will take this week to begin creating your peaceful home:

_____

_____

_____

What are some ways you will make it easier for those in your home to express their needs?

_____

_____

_____

_____

CHAPTER 7
COMMON BARRIERS TO ACHIEVING PEACE AT HOME

THE FAMILIAR ROBERT BURNS QUOTE, "BEST LAID PLANS ...often go awry," is certainly appropriate here. To your efforts in establishing a peaceful home, add patience. Patience with yourself and with others. Achieving lasting peace at home is a task as challenging as it is valuable. This book has tried to present a simple model for ease of application but it is important to note the barriers you may encounter along the way so that you will know how to move past them.

FAVORITISM

Even if you think favoritism does not exist in your home, it can make a world of difference in your family relationships if you address it. Give your loved ones the gift of peace of mind and let them know you think they are all special and that they are all just as important to you. It sounds corny but, I highly recommend sitting everyone down, having a conversation, and letting them know, ver- bally, that no one is more important than anyone else in your home. Follow it up by letting them know they are individually precious, unique, and valuable. Then let your actions reflect your words in the day to day way you treat them. This will do wonders for lowering the anxiety level in your home and reducing conflict. When your kids find out that they don't have to compete for your love, and that no one is better than anyone else, they will instantly be re- lieved. Heck, they might just curl up into a ball and fall fast asleep. It is sooo relaxing and relieving to know that you don't need to compete for love and that someone thinks you're just as important as everyone else. It is AMAZING.

There are a few reasons favoritism exists in some homes. The first is personality. Our personalities naturally find ease with other complimentary personalities. If someone in your home is easier for you to relate to or to understand, unconscious favoritism may develop. Of course, it is fine to feel this way but, the problem comes when we allow it to influence our beliefs and actions, when we mis-in- terpret ease as "better than." Unaddressed or unchecked, favoritism can grow to be very unhealthy for everyone in the family. If this situation exists in your family, recognizing it and adjusting your behaviors to be more equitable with each family member will be very important. Favoritism naturally creates anxiety in those who are not "the favorite" and therefore conflict will be ever present.

Favoritism may exist in one's home as the result of a parental lack of energy. Some personalities in our family may require more energy from us as we try to build and maintain relationship. When tired, we may lean more heavily on the relationships and personalities we find to be easier. Protecting our energy so that we can engage with each member of our family equally is important for maintaining peace in the home. Do you find yourself spending less time with those whose personalities are not as easy for you? Though challenging, those individuals are in need of a healthy relationship with you just as much as everyone else.

Another reason favoritism may exist within a family is simply that of tradition. Perhaps you grew up in a home where the oldest child received way more praise and attention than any other children. Perhaps you grew up in a home where any one child in particular, for whatever reason, was a favorite. If this is the case, having a favorite may seem normal to you and the existence of a family favorite may be passed down from generation to generation as a sort of unspoken tradition. The harm a tradition such as this can create in a family is not to be underestimated. A continued tradition of favoritism leaves behind a legacy of anxiety, pain, insecurity, broken relationships, and conflict. If you want to achieve lasting peace in your home and in your relationships, and if you want everyone in your home to become the healthiest version of themselves, the tradition of favoritism must end with you.

COMPETITION

When we understand the relationship between unmet needs and conflict—or the fear/anxiety of unmet needs and how it contributes to conflict—the whole notion of competitiveness gets flipped on its head. Competition is good for achieving personal bests, inspiring creativity, and motivating innovation; however, when competition is used or required to meet needs, we insist on the presence of conflict in our homes and in our society. The dynamics of competition require that some win and some lose. This dynamic is counterproductive to meeting human needs. Since we all share the same needs, a win/lose dynamic means that some will not get their needs met and conflict is inevitable. Not having needs met invariably causes dysfunction within the self and therefore, in relationships, families, and society.

It is at this point that we confront long standing ideo-
logical differences regarding whether or not it is possible
for humans to have all of their needs met. According to
the Center for Non-Violent Communication and others
who study peacemaking initiatives, the answer is yes. Yes,
it is possible for you to have all of your needs met. It is
not achieved overnight but, it is certainly possible to work
toward and achieve having one's needs met. The primary
issue we all face, and that elicits conflict, is that we often
do not know how to get our needs met. As humans, we
tend to have a few finite solutions in our minds about how
we will go about getting our needs met when, in fact, there
may be infinitely more ways to do so. Later in this book,
we will review ideas for getting needs met in peaceful and
productive ways.

Peace is possible. Getting everyone's natural human
needs met, is possible. Competition hinders that process.
Re-examining our understanding and use of competition
is critical if we are to achieve peace in our homes.

Whether you consider your family to be competitive
people or not, this dynamic exists in most homes to varying
degrees. It may be a healthy competition that challenges
individuals to be the best version of themselves or, it may
be unhealthy competition used to get needs met and protect the self.

Individuals, especially children, often confuse being great at a particular skill with being a great person and having personal value. We all have a need to be valued, to matter (see the NVC needs list provided in chapter 3). We all have the need to be seen and heard, as well. Having these needs met contributes to our sense of well-being and security. When personal value relies on performance, this real human need can only be met through competition and domination. When personal value is recognized as innate, the need to be valued is met through relationship, contribution, and collaboration.

Our motivation to achieve starts at home. Home is where our values are first formed and molded. If we grew up in a home where being better than others met our need for value, then competition was necessary. If we grew up in a home where our value was recognized as innate, then our need for value was met through relationship, contribution, and collaboration. When a family collaborates in an effort to meet the needs of its members, conflict cannot thrive. It is extinguished and peace at home can flourish.

While it is true that our society values competition for its ability to motivate creativity and innovation, competition undermines communities and invites conflict when individuals and groups focus on being "better than" versus doing their best for the good of self and community.

We can greatly reduce conflict at home and in our communities when we embrace equity, recognize innate value, and acknowledge, "I am important and so are you."

LACK OF COMMUNICATION SKILLS

Underdeveloped communication skills can present a challenge along your journey to creating a peaceful home. Children, in particular, have a difficult time accessing and expressing their concerns because they have limited vocabulary and limited practice when it comes to self-reflection. When relating to anyone with underdeveloped communication skills, paying attention to their behavior, and suspending judgement, will be much more important. Behavior is how they will first attempt to express a concern. Providing individuals in your home with a feelings list or needs list can be a very practical way of assisting them in expressing their concerns and anxieties about unmet needs. Giving individuals the words and the space to practice self-expression is key to moving peace forward in your home—not to mention helping everyone involved to grow personally.

There is a popular piece of information (source unknown) floating around the internet that attempts to interpret some common behaviors. It reads as follows:

- Kids who **whine** usually feel powerless and like they can't cope; they often just need a chance to cry.

- Kids who are **bossy** and **controlling** worry that they won't get their needs met.
- Kids who **taunt** or **compete** with siblings often need to feel more valued for who they are, and more connected to parent.
- Kids who **don't listen** often feel their desires are not acknowledged.
- Kids who **rebel** usually need a chance to feel more powerful and competent.
- Kids who **disrespect** you are always showing you they don't feel connected enough to you.

The previous examples can be applied to adults just as easily. These are all very real needs.. mourning, collaboration, value, acknowledgement, competence, connection. They are also needs that children, and many adults, find difficult to communicate verbally. It is especially difficult to verbally express a need to be heard/acknowledged because the very nature of the problem is a barrier. Behavior, often negative, is a common (and effective) way of attempting to communicate this need.

FALSE HUMILITY

What is false humility and how is it a barrier to peace in the home? False humility describes behavior often used to hide or discourage personal pride because we fear appearing arrogant and we fear others' reactions to our success. Rather than demonstrating healthy self-love and personal pride, we hide behind false humility impeding our ability to meet our needs, creating internal conflict, and interfering with our ability to relate authentically with others.

False humility is a protective behavior that can be a barrier to creating a peaceful home by its inauthenticity and dishonesty. It also prevents us from meeting our own needs for personal pride and self-acceptance. We may think we are protecting others by behaving with false humility but in doing so we deprive them of the opportunity to witness healthy self-love, self-acceptance, and pride. Pride is often mistaken for arrogance and interpreted as a negative quality. Arrogance is believing oneself to be better than others and certainly contributes to conflict. Pride, however, is liking yourself and, liking yourself can only improve your life and the lives of those around you.

Expressing and enjoying personal pride may also be mis-interpreted as showing off but, telling the world we love ourselves is actually very important! It sets an example and allows others the freedom to love themselves, too. As our society learns to love and accept the self more, we will see insecurities diminish and the negative, sometimes violent, behaviors that accompany insecurity will decrease.

CONFLICT AS A MEANS TO CONNECTION

It is common for negative behaviors to be a misguided attempt at achieving a rather harmless goal. When we have a need that we want to meet, it does not necessarily mean that we understand how to best meet the need. We may try several different methods, many of which are unsuccessful, such as self-sabotaging or behaviors that result in hurting others. Connection, for example, is a human need that is elusive to many of us. We want to experience a real connection with another human being yet, because of different communication styles, cultural norms, nurturing experiences, love languages, etc., many of us are completely in the dark as to how to appropriately and successfully connect with other human beings. It can be particularly troubling when we grew up in an emotionally unavailable home environment. In these environments, we learn dysfunctional ways of connecting. One such dysfunctional method is through conflict. If we received little attention at home, we may have used conflict to get the attention and connection we needed. This book focuses on reducing conflict but, it will be much more difficult to do if you or those around you are in the habit of using conflict to connect. Even though conflict is difficult and not enjoyable, it often gives us an outlet to express emotions or concerns that may be difficult for us to express in other dynamics. The self-expression, energy, and personal attention involved in conflict can leave us feeling closer to the individual with whom we are in conflict. In these instances, eliminating conflict can feel like eliminating our only means of accessing connection and, that can be scary. Again, connection is a need and if conflict is the only way we know how to meet it, we will instinctively try to preserve conflict as a way to meet that need. If this is something you recognize in yourself or in your family, it is a good idea to seek professional help to overcome the issue and to find other ways of connecting. You may even notice this affecting your relationships outside of the home, such as with friends or at work. In particular, this behavior may resemble what people refer to as "authority issues." If you feel the only way to connect with or feel seen by your boss is to engage in conflict, you may find it difficult to maintain long term employment. There is hope for dysfunctional habits that are used to meet needs. More effective behaviors and ways of getting our needs met can be learned. Having help and accountability is very important. If you want to achieve peace in your home, you will need to study the conflict dynamics in your home to see if conflict is being used as a way to meet a need.

LACK OF BOUNDARIES

If the concept of boundaries is unfamiliar to you, it may be difficult to identify boundaries in your day to day life. A good way to start recognizing boundaries is to simply listen for, or use, the word "no." "No" is the most basic of boundaries. It draws an invisible line to mark off the limits of what is acceptable to us and what is not. Boundaries are a functional, healthy way of communicating our needs. The day I came to realize the importance of boundaries was the day I grew fed up with not having my own boundaries respected. I learned that if I wanted others to respect my boundaries, I needed to start respecting theirs. This concept was the impetus to a massive shift I experienced in my ability to reduce the amount of conflict in my life. When I started respecting others' "no" (remember there are many dysfunctional ways we attempt to meet our needs), I had to start using more functional ways of getting my needs met. At the same time, I became more aware of those individuals in my life who were good at respecting my "no's" and of those who were not. This gave me great clarity as to those with whom I would spend my time and those relationships that would need to change or end.

A lack of boundaries within the home prevents peace and indicates that individuals do not know how to effectively express or meet their needs. Attempts to express or meet needs will be poorly communicated, dysfunctional, and desperate. This typically results in conflict and crisis. Learning to express needs in a functional way and, to collaborate to get them met, is key to reducing conflict in the home and in relationships. Using the NVC needs list and feelings list is a great way to begin the work of improving communication of needs and problem solving to meet them. Further study on boundaries and counsel from therapeutic professionals is also recommended. *For additional assistance regarding boundary setting, see the resource list at the back of this book.*

CHAPTER 7 EXERCISE:

What barriers to creating a peaceful home exist in your life and relationships?

_____

_____

_____

_____

How will you address these barriers and work to remove them?

_____

_____

_____

_____

CHAPTER 8
LOOKING FORWARD

W E'VE DISCUSSED FROM WHERE CONFLICT AND NEGA-tive behaviors arise, the unmet needs behind them, and the various barriers you may face along your journey to creating a peaceful home.

You now understand the steps involved in working through a conflict. It is a rather simple process but, ap-plying it takes effort. Remember, the process of peace is not a passive process. It requires sincere interest in helping others to meet their needs, a willingness to see the world from different perspectives, and empathy. As you put the concepts in this book into practice, I am confident that you will begin to see a dramatic change in the amount of peace you experience at home and in your relationships.

These concepts are powerful. Once you observe them working in the smaller day to day disharmonies of life, you will begin to see how they might apply to larger scenarios and more difficult experiences. Proceed with caution. Discuss what you are learning with others who are on the same journey. There is great healing to be found, great courage required, and always great empathy to give. You must decide how far these concepts will take you and how much you will allow them to transform your life and relationships.

It is not lost on me that the concepts and ideas in this book may be controversial when considering more difficult and painful life experiences and conflicts. When our lives have been severely disrupted or we have been greatly injured by an individual seeking to meet their needs in dysfunctional and desperate ways, it is natural to be angry. It is hard to accept that some individuals would attempt to meet their needs by hurting others. In these situations, we might consider the possibility that such individuals felt their needs could not be met in any other way—via functional or non-hurtful means—and that desperation was present. Though not excusable, and certainly not without consequence, these actions exist and, according to the models we have been discussing, negative behaviors are born from traumatic events or anxious thoughts about unmet needs. It is much easier for us to assume a position that refuses to see the humanity of such individuals and to ascribe to them an "enemy image." If you are not ready to consider such things, it is okay. Some things are too difficult. We can continue the work of peacemaking to whatever extent we are able.

UNDERSTANDING ANXIETY

When it comes to meeting needs, it makes sense that anxiety would be present. It is a natural instinct to ensure our health and safety needs are being met. People experience different levels of anxiety and this may be due to earlier life experiences where needs were not met or were difficult to meet. Just understanding what our needs are and knowing it is okay for us to pursue meeting them brings relief.

In my work teaching non-violent crisis intervention at a behavioral health hospital and in an addiction treatment setting, I learned a great deal about these issues. What stood out to me most, throughout all of my training and work, was that anxiety and trauma were at the root of these mental and behavioral health issues. Where addiction and mental illness have baffled humanity for centuries, recent research and scientific studies increasingly identify anxiety as the underlying cause for the majority of these illnesses. A world of healing possibilities opens up when we know where to begin the work and where the source of pain lies. When we make the observation that anxiety is not only at the core of mental health and addiction issues, but also related to physical and relational well-being, we see everyone we know differently and, we understand how very important it is that humanity turn to address the issue of anxiety.

There is much more that can be said about these topics and more research shared. For further information about the connection between addiction and anxiety, health and anxiety, or anxiety management, check out additional Peaceful Home books and resources online.

CHAPTER 8 EXERCISE:

The space below has been provided for you to reflect and debrief on your experience with the ideas presented in this book.

INDEX I.
SUGGESTIONS FOR MEETING NEEDS...

MEETING YOUR NEEDS FOR CONNECTION:

- Joining a club or group of those with similar interests
- Finding friends who share your values
- Choosing friends who have earned your trust
- Attending a support group
- Meeting with a Counselor or Therapist
- Pursuing your interests and loves
- Joining a gym
- Picking a favorite coffee shop or other spot
- Choosing people and environments where you feel welcome and appreciated
- Volunteering with others to meet a common goal
- Inviting others to share their ideas
- Being flexible and willing to consider others' points of view
- Scheduling regular calls, walks, or meetups
- Taking a communication course
- Enrolling in any class of your interest
- Inviting guests over or out for dinner
- Investing in people who invest in you

MEETING YOUR NEEDS FOR PHYSICAL WELL-BEING:

- Taking responsibility for your own well-being
- Selecting a home in which you feel safe
- Making self-care a priority
- Reflecting on your needs
- Planning ahead to meet needs
- Using a calendar to help you plan
- Visiting a career center at a local college
- Utilizing community resources for housing assistance
- Utilizing community resources for food assistance
- Researching assistance programs for healthcare
- Leaving dangerous or unhealthy situations
- Accessing a library or county agency for support
- Deciding you deserve health, safety, and peace
- Believing you are worth it
- Accepting self and acknowledging personal value
- Reaching out for help without shame
- Asking for a hug from a trusted friend
- Choosing to respect yourself regardless of past-choices or circumstance
- Using functional, positive, and non-harmful strategies to meet your needs

MEETING YOUR NEEDS FOR HONESTY:

- Telling yourself the truth, even when it is hard
- Acknowledging your needs and desires
- Mourning your unmet needs
- Acknowledging dysfunctional strategies used when attempting to meet needs
- Choosing to be the person you want to be
- Accepting imperfection
- Being true to yourself, your values, and standards
- Living with integrity
- Addressing and problem solving for unmet needs
- Asking for help with unmet needs
- Joining a support group
- Finding accountability and holding self accountable
- Taking responsibility for choices and behaviors

MEETING YOUR NEEDS FOR AUTONOMY:

- Taking responsibility for meeting needs of self
- Setting appropriate boundaries with others
- Being assertive when expressing my needs
- Utilizing my freedom to choose for myself
- Thinking for myself
- Taking responsibility for my choices and behaviors
- Not taking responsibility for others' choices and behaviors
- Determining how much space I need
- Deciding what I will do, how, and when
- Accepting what I cannot change and changing what I can
- Using functional, positive, and non-harmful strategies to pursue my needs and wants
- Making decisions based upon my needs and not based on others' emotions
- Making time for self and self-care

MEETING YOUR NEEDS FOR PLAY:

- Acknowledging your need for joy and humor
- Making time to relax
- Encouraging laughter
- Becoming more comfortable with happiness and peace
- Allowing self to rest
- Accepting feelings of peace and contentment
- Setting time aside to appreciate and enjoy
- Identifying your favorite things to do
- Choosing entertainment that does not harm self or others
- Using functional, positive, and non-harmful strategies to meet your need for play
- Organizing fun activities
- Joining a community sports team or hobby group
- Hosting special party nights, bbqs, picnics, etc.

MEETING YOUR NEEDS FOR PEACE:

- Finding community where you feel a sense of equality
- Participating in a group with a common goal
- Looking for beautiful places to rest and relax
- Appreciating beauty in art or nature
- Organizing or cleaning your environment
- Simplifying your life
- Using functional, positive, and non-harmful strategies to reduce number of responsibilities
- Learning to meditate
- Engaging in a flow activity such as cooking, crafting, cleaning, creating, or tending.
- Scheduling time to be alone
- Designating quiet times
- Playing peaceful music
- Scheduling time to relax each day
- Working with a mediator
- Learning about non-violent communication
- Practicing guided relaxation

MEETING YOUR NEEDS FOR MEANING:

- Pursuing your interests
- Educating self
- Identifying personal strengths
- Contributing to community
- Noting what excites you
- Noticing what activities boost your self-respect and self-appreciation
- Making time for self-discovery
- Participating in creative projects
- Developing competence in areas of interest
- Seeking opportunities to experience small successes
- Using opportunities for self-expression
- Embracing challenges as opportunities to grow
- Participating in volunteer activities
- Sharing your expertise with others
- Celebrating success and achievement
- Acknowledging and mourning loss
- Creating traditions and rituals to honor things of value and importance

These are only some of the many positive strategies we can use to meet our needs. For additional ideas and resources, please connect with the Peaceful Home community online at

peacefulhomesolutions.com

Please use this book as a resource to refer back to whenever you need it and share it with those you love. I hope you found the concepts to be as helpful and transformative as I have. Thank you for reading *Achieving Peace at Home*. If you enjoyed this book, or received value from it, your review on Amazon would be greatly appreciated!

RECOMMENDED RESOURCES

Look for future releases from Amy Mikal and Peaceful Home at Amazon or PeacefulHomeSolutions.com.

ADDITIONAL RECOMMENDATIONS

- *Changes That Heal* by Dr. Henry Cloud
- *Boundaries* by Henry Cloud & John Townsend
- *Boundaries with Children* by Henry Cloud & John Townsend
- *Boundaries in Marriage* by Henry Cloud & John Townsend

WORKS CITED

Long, N. J., Wood, M. M., & Fecser, F. A. (2001). *Life space crisis intervention: Talking with students in conflict* (2nd ed.). PRO-ED

Enhancing Verbal Skills Training, CPI Non-Violent Crisis Intervention

Needs and Feelings Inventory Lists, Center for Non-Violent Communication

Nonviolent Communication, Marshall Rosenberg

Psychiatric diagnoses, trauma, and suicidality, Silje K Floen, Ask Elklit. Ann Gen Psychiatry. 2007; 6: 12. Published online 2007 Apr 20. doi: 10.1186/1744-859X-6-12

Rosenberg, M. B. (1999). *Nonviolent communication: A language of compassion.* Del Mar, CA: PuddleDancer Press

Made in the USA
Monee, IL
26 September 2020

42749132R00055